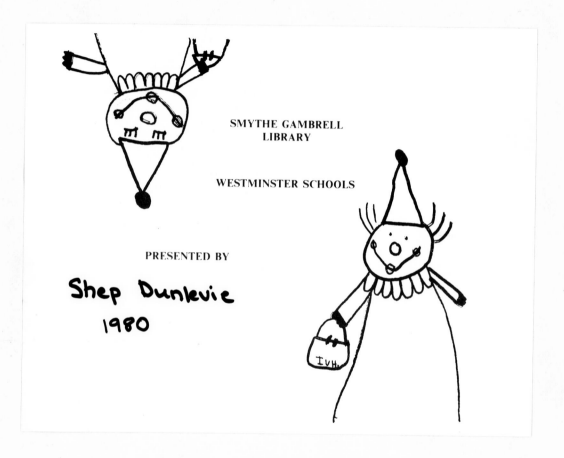

SMYTHE GAMBRELL
LIBRARY

WESTMINSTER SCHOOLS

PRESENTED BY

Shep Dunkuie
1980

A January Fog Will Freeze a Hog

and Other Weather Folklore

A January Fog Will Freeze a Hog

and Other Weather Folklore

Compiled and Edited by **Hubert Davis**

Illustrated by **John Wallner**

CROWN PUBLISHERS, INC., NEW YORK

At the back of this book you will find information about each weather rhyme, listed according to first lines.

Text copyright © 1977 by Hubert J. Davis.
Illustrations copyright © 1977 by John Wallner.
All rights reserved. No part of this publication may be reproduced, stored in a retrieval system, or transmitted, in any form or by any means, electronic, mechanical, photocopying, recording, or otherwise, without prior written permission of the publisher. Inquiries should be addressed to Crown Publishers, Inc., One Park Avenue, New York, N.Y. 10016.
Manufactured in the United States of America.
Published simultaneously in Canada by General Publishing Company Limited.
10 9 8 7 6 5 4 3

The text of this book is set in Palatino. The illustrations are black and white line and wash reproduced in halftone.

Library of Congress Cataloging in Publication Data
Main entry under title:
A January fog will freeze a hog, and other weather folklore.
   Summary: Thirty sayings used to predict the weather are accompanied by a factual explanation, the origin of the saying, and its general reliability.
   1. Weather lore—United States—Juvenile literature.
[1. Weather lore] I. Davis, Hubert J. II. Wallner, John C.
QC998.J36 1977   551.6'31'0973   76-54333
ISBN 0-517-52811-8

For Ruby

The Cherokee Indians
Used to note
The rainbow as the hem
Of their Sun God's coat.

When sheep gather in a huddle,
Tomorrow we'll have a puddle.

Expect the weather to be fair
When crows fly in pairs.

A circle around the moon,
'Twill rain soon.

When ladybugs swarm,
Expect a day that's warm.

When the cow scratches her ear
It means a shower is near;

But when she thumps her ribs with her tail
Expect thunder, lightning, and hail.

The owls hoot, peacocks toot,
The ducks quack, frogs yak—
'Twill rain.
The loons call, swallows fall,
Chickens hover, groundhogs take cover—
'Twill rain.

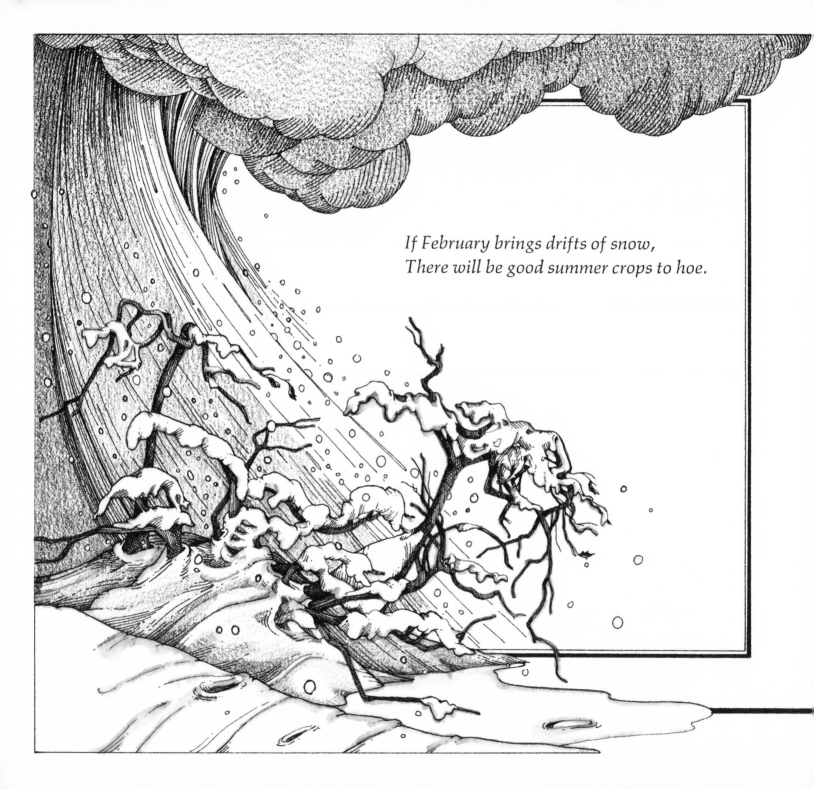

If February brings drifts of snow,
There will be good summer crops to hoe.

When clouds look like black smoke,
A wise man will put on his cloak.

Rainbow in the morning,
Shepherds take warning.

Rainbow at night,
Shepherd's delight.

When the wind is out of the east,
'Tis good for neither man nor beast.

But when the wind is out of the west,
It sends every man the very best.

If the rooster crows at night,
He's trying to say rain's in sight.

If wild geese go out to sea,
Good weather there will surely be.

When chickens scratch together
There's sure to be foul weather.

Fog on the hills,
More water for the mills.

When crickets slow down their ticks,
When pigs in their mouths carry sticks,
When ladybugs try to swarm,
The animals together
Foretell the weather.

A cloud as if it had been
Scratched by a hen—
Get ready to haul your topsails in.

The hooting of an owl
Says the weather will be foul.

When mist comes from the hill,
Good weather it doth spill;

When mist comes from the sea,
Bad weather there will be.

Wind before rain,
Fair weather again.

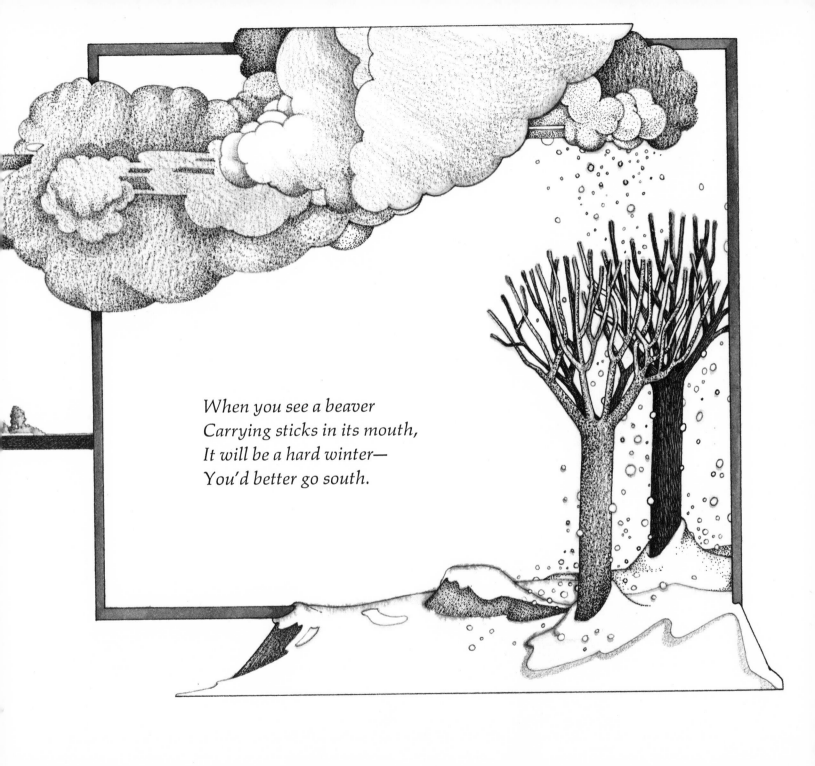

When you see a beaver
Carrying sticks in its mouth,
It will be a hard winter—
You'd better go south.

When clouds appear
Like rocks and towers,
The earth will be washed
By frequent showers.

Crow on the fence,
Rain will come down;
Rain will go hence
When crow's on the ground.

When bees far away
Make their flight,
Days will be warm and skies bright.

But when their flight
Ends near home,
Stormy weather is sure to come.

Thunder in the morning,
All day storming.

Thunder at night,
Traveler's delight.

*I know ladies by the score
Whose hair foretells the storm;
Long before it begins to pour
Their curls take a drooping form.*

When the chairs squeak,
It's about rain they speak.

The crow with loud cries
A sudden shower foretells;
In single file they fly
Up and over the hills.

On a cold snowy day
Country folks say:
The old woman is picking her geese,
Selling feathers penny apiece.

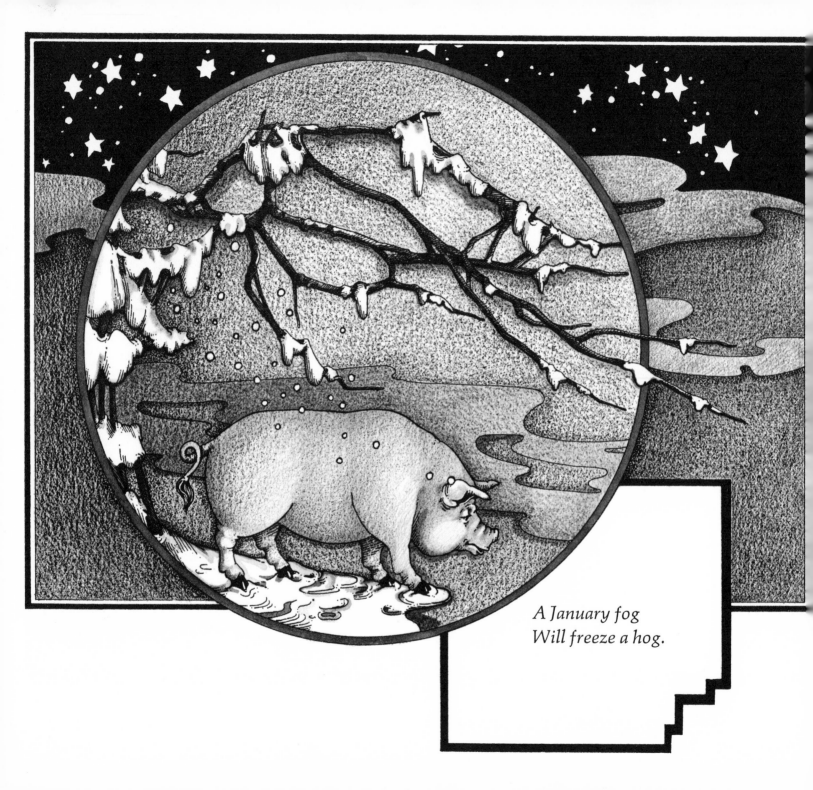

A January fog
Will freeze a hog.

A long time ago, people didn't have radios, television sets, newspapers, or meteorologists to give them the weather forecast. When they wanted to find out about the weather, they looked carefully for signs that would show them how the weather was going to change. They noticed the color of the sky and the shapes of the clouds; they remembered where rainbows had appeared when the weather changed and how the sun and the moon looked before and after a thunderstorm or a snowfall. They also looked to see how animals behaved as the weather and the seasons changed. Then they made up simple little verses about what they observed. The verses they made were usually short and easy to remember. Some of them were just fun and nonsense, but many accurately gauged the environmental signs that help the weatherman make his forecasts today.

Some of the people who came to the New World a long time ago settled in Canada, some in New England, and others scattered throughout the rest of the United States. They brought with them weather rhymes their grandparents had made up. But since the weather is different in different regions of the world, they made up new rhymes of their own and changed some of the older ones to fit the different climate, plant, and animal life that they encountered in America.

The Cherokee Indians...

The Cherokee Indians believed that their Sun God, dressed in golden robes, drove away storms. He rode on a swift eagle, moving so fast that the multicolored hem of his robe was spread from the tip of one eagle wing to the other in a huge semicircle. Found especially in the South.

When sheep gather in a huddle...

Sheep are sensitive to small, telltale changes in the weather, because their wool traps air as insulation. Sheep huddle to keep warm, so may foretell the coming of cool air and rain. Found in the South and in New England; a good weather indicator.

Expect the weather to be fair...

Crows feed in groups, but they seek shelter and roost in separate places. Therefore, when we see them flying together in pairs, they are not likely to be seeking shelter, and we can expect the weather to be fair. Found in New England, southern United States, and England; a fair indicator of weather.

A circle around the moon...

The high, feathery, diffuse clouds that create haloes around the moon (and the sun) are cirrostratus clouds, made entirely of ice crystals. Ice crystals refract light differently from water droplets and thus give rise to the circles mentioned here, in some places also known as a "Cock's Eye." While these clouds themselves do not cause precipitation, they are frequently the first stages of an approaching storm and may themselves become more water-laden clouds at a lower altitude. Found in Virginia, North Carolina, throughout the U.S., and Scotland; a reliable indicator of stormy weather approaching.

When ladybugs swarm...

Ladybug beetles are covered by a set of hard wings which hold in heat. They fly about as a means of cooling off when the weather begins to get warm. Because they do not have a constant internal body temperature, all insects respond to warm weather and fly more easily. Found especially in the southern states and in the Appalachian Mountains; this is a fair predictor of weather.

When the cow scratches her ear...

The hairs inside a cow's ear respond to the changes that come before rain (low atmospheric pressure and increased humidity) and may cause her to scratch. Before a violent thunderstorm, static charges of electricity can cause a cow's hair to stand out. To relieve this discomfort, a cow may continuously brush herself with her tail. Found generally in the South, Scotland, and England; a fair predictor of weather.

The owls hoot, peacocks toot...

Most animals are more sensitive than we are to changes in the pressure, temperature, and humidity of the air. Some changes in the weather, such as the low pressure and increased humidity before a storm, may make animals uncomfortable, restless, and noisy. Their behavior tells us that the weather is soon to change. Found in Virginia, Kentucky, England, and Scotland; a reliable indicator that weather will change.

If February brings drifts of snow...

During a very cold, snowy winter, some weed seeds are damaged, many insect larvae are killed, and an abundance of water is stored in the ground. Later, the scarcity of weeds and insects which might otherwise damage crops, in addition to the abundance of water available to young plants, provides good conditions for crop growth and increases the chances for a rich harvest. Found in the mountainous regions of the South; a reliable predictor.

When clouds look like black smoke...

This describes several cloud patterns which may produce rain or snow: flat, gray, altostratus clouds, which form in one or more layers, and may cause rain or snow. When altostratus clouds thicken and drift lower, they form the dark, heavy, ragged nimbostratus clouds from which continuous rain or snow falls. Cumulus clouds may build up to a towering cumulonimbus formation, bringing a thunderstorm. Found in Virginia, North Carolina, Kentucky, Scotland, and in parts of England; a very reliable weather forecaster.

Rainbow in the morning...

When rain clouds filled with moisture are in the west and the morning sun shines on them from the east, a rainbow is created. The water droplets in the clouds scatter the sunlight, causing the colors of the spectrum to show. Although storms arise and travel in different patterns, many of our storms move from west to east, so a shepherd (or anyone observing such a rainbow) might expect rain when the clouds reached him. In the evening, when the setting sun shines on rain clouds in the east and makes a rainbow, this indicates that the clouds have already passed overhead and there will be no rain. Found generally throughout the United States; a reliable weather indicator.

When the wind is out of the east...

Winds blow constantly over the face of the earth, in complicated, changing patterns. Some winds from the east, known as polar easterlies, are very cold, originating from the frozen icy regions of the earth's poles. (In England, a cold persistent wind that blows down from the east during winter has been said to bring depression and moodiness to the British people.) Since a wind blowing out of the east is blowing in the direction opposite from the one in which the earth is moving, a storm carried by an easterly wind would spread as time passes. Winds out of the west are warmer. Since westerly winds blow in the same direction as the earth is moving, a storm pushed by such a wind would soon dissipate. Found generally throughout the United States, England, and Scotland; a reliable weather forecaster.

If the rooster crows at night...

Roosters feel the changes in pressure, temperature, and humidity of the air because their feathers act as insulation. The changes in air pressure, humidity, and temperature that precede a storm may make the rooster restless, uncomfortable, and cause him to crow at night. Found in the South and in New England; a good weather indicator.

If wild geese go out to sea...

Ducks, geese, and other birds are very sensitive to changes in atmospheric conditions. They would probably head out to sea in fair weather and take shelter if a storm was brewing. Found in Virginia, North Carolina, and New England; a reliable weather indicator.

When chickens scratch together...

Since chickens' feathers trap air (as insulation), they quickly feel the changes in air pressure, moisture, and temperature that come before a storm. These changes may be sufficient to make them restless, move about more, or scratch together to keep warm. Found in the South and in New England; a good weather indicator.

Fog on the hills...

Fogs on hills are really low-hanging clouds that form as warm moist air blows against the slope of a hill or mountain and is forced upward. As the air rises, it expands and cools, and the moisture in the air condenses into droplets. If the fog does not evaporate, it may later cause rain. Found generally in Virginia, North Carolina, and in mountainous sections of New England, and Scotland; only a moderately reliable weather predictor.

When crickets slow down their ticks...

The temperature, pressure, and amount of moisture in the air (humidity) change as the weather changes. Animals and insects are more sensitive to small changes in the weather than we are, and their behavior may reflect the coming of rain, snow, or warm weather. Found in Virginia, North Carolina, Kentucky, England, and Scotland; a reliable indicator that weather is about to change.

A cloud as if it had been...

This is a cloud pattern, the high, wispy, feathery cirrus formation, which signals that rain may fall within twenty-four hours. Found in Virginia, North Carolina, Kentucky, Scotland, and in parts of England; a reliable weather forecaster.

The hooting of an owl...

Birds feel small changes in pressure, temperature, and amount of moisture in the air (humidity) because their feathers act as insulation by trapping and holding air. The low pressure and increased humidity that come before a storm may make the owl somewhat uncomfortable, more active, or cause him to hoot more. Found throughout the South and in New England; a good weather indicator.

When mist comes from the hill...

Mists or fogs on the tops of hills are usually shallow and do not have enough moisture to produce rain. They are easily dissipated by the sun's heat as the day progresses. Mists from lakes, broad rivers, and the oceans, however, contain much more water, making rain more likely. Many sea fogs are the result of the condensation that occurs when warm, moist air blows over water that is cooler than the air. When large quantities of warm, moist air blow over water that has a lower temperature, the resulting fog can be quite thick and hazardous. Found in New England and especially the coastal states; a reliable weather forecaster.

Wind before rain...

When a noticeable wind precedes rain, this indicates that the rain clouds are being pushed by the wind. Since the clouds are moved by the wind, the storm ought to pass soon. Found in New England, Virginia and other parts of the South; a reliable weather indicator.

When you see a beaver...

The idea of beavers carrying sticks in preparation for winter was borrowed from the Indians who believed that beavers carried sticks to build better homes before a harsh winter arrived. This belief is common throughout the Northeast and South, especially among the mountain people of the Appalachians, but it is not a reliable weather indicator.

When clouds appear...

Clouds appear when invisible water vapor in the air condenses around tiny particles of dust, forming small water droplets or ice crystals. Clouds can take various formations depending on the amount of moisture they contain, their altitude, and wind and temperature conditions. The cumulus formation (from the Latin word *cumulus*, meaning mound or heap) has a dark, flat base and a characteristic cauliflower shape, as though billowing, domelike clouds had been piled atop one another. Cumulus clouds sometimes build up to form the towering, mountainous cumulonimbus clouds, or thunderclouds, referred to here. These clouds generally produce showers of rain, snow, hail, or thunderstorms. Found in Virginia, North Carolina, Kentucky, Scotland, and England; a very reliable weather forecaster.

Crow on the fence...

Crows are ground feeders, much like robins. After a rain, they are likely to find an abundance of food, because the rainwater forces worms and other insects out of the ground. Found in Virginia, North Carolina, Tennessee, northeastern United States, and England; not a reliable forecaster of weather.

When bees far away...

All insects, and bees in particular, are sensitive to changes in heat, humidity, and air pressure. When it is likely to rain, the air pressure decreases, the humidity increases; sensitive to this, bees stay near their hives. Found in Virginia, Kentucky, North Carolina, and England; this is a reliable weather indicator.

Thunder in the morning...

Thunder is the sound that follows a flash of lightning, caused by the explosive effect lightning has on the air. The electrical discharge along the lightning stroke heats the air so rapidly that there is a violent expansion of air, producing a wave. This wave is heard as the crash of thunder. Thunder is just one part of a violent storm containing enormous amounts of energy that we see and feel as rain, lightning, wind, and sometimes hail. Thunder can be heard at a distance, although the storm of which it's a part may not pass overhead. Thunder heard in the morning would affect a traveler's daytime plans; thunder heard in the evening would not, since most thunderstorms are over in a matter of hours, and fair weather is likely to follow. Found generally throughout the United States; a very reliable forecaster of weather.

I know ladies by the score...

Human hair responds in a very sensitive manner to the amount of moisture (humidity) in the air. Although naturally curly hair becomes more curly in wet weather, straight hair that has been waved or curled becomes straight again. Strands of human hair are often used in devices (hygrometers) that measure the change in humidity. Found everywhere; a reliable indicator of weather change.

When the chairs squeak...

During dry weather, wooden chairs give up some of their moisture to the dry air. As rain approaches and the air becomes increasingly humid, the wood in turn absorbs moisture from the air. As it does so, it expands, causing the chairs to creak. (For similar reasons, wooden doors and drawers may expand unevenly and warp during wet weather.) Found throughout the South, in New England, and Scotland; a reliable indicator of changing weather conditions.

The crow with loud cries...

Crows usually feed together in groups but roost and seek shelter individually, in separate places. They would fly away in single file when a storm approaches. Found in Virginia, North Carolina, Tennessee, the northeastern United States, and some parts of England; a fairly reliable weather forecaster.

On a cold snowy day...

This is just a cute little rhyme and has no scientific basis or value. Found throughout the United States.

A January fog...

Fog is a cloud whose base touches the ground, and, like a cloud, fog is composed of small droplets of water or, in very cold regions, ice crystals. Cold moist air is more penetrating than cold dry air; a fog of ice crystals would freeze most any animal. Found throughout the South and in New England; a rhyme for fun, not meant as a weather forecaster.